# Can you see us?

# Can you see me?

Yes, I can see you.

Can you see me?

Yes, we can see you.

Can you see me?

Yes, we can see you.

We can all see Dad.

Oxford Reading Tree

# Hide and Seek

Roderick Hunt

Alex Brychta

Story written by Roderick Hunt
Illustrations by Alex Brychta

Oxford
Reading
Tree

## What's this story about?

The children are playing hide and seek in the garden. Who is the last to be found?

## Talk together

Read the title on the cover and talk about the game of hide and seek. Ask, "Who is hiding? Who is seeking?"

## Read the story

**W** = Word recognition **C** = Language comprehension

- **W** Begin to read the story together.
- **C** Page 1, talk about what Wilf is doing (counting down).
- **W** Point out the tricky word 'you' and help the child to read it. Can the child see who is hiding?
- **C** Pages 2 and 3, ask, "Who did Wilf find first?" Help the child to read the question and the answer.
- **C** Pages 6 and 7, notice what is happening to Dad, then ask, "How do you think the story will end?"
- **W** Page 8, point to the tricky word 'all'. Ask the child to tell you some words that rhyme with 'all'.
- **C** Ask the child to read the whole story independently.